CORNERSTONES OF FREEDOM™

P9-DHQ-402

The REVOLUTIONARY WAR

BY JOSH GREGORY

CHILDREN'S PRESS®
An Imprint of Scholastic Inc.
New York Toronto London Auckland Sydney
Mexico City New Delhi Hong Kong
Danbury, Connecticut

BRINGING HISTORY to LIFE

Content Consultant
Evan Haefeli, PhD
Assistant Professor of History
Columbia University
New York, New York

Library of Congress Cataloging-in-Publication Data

Gregory, Josh.
  The Revolutionary War/by Josh Gregory.
    p. cm.—(Cornerstones of freedom)
  Includes bibliographical references and index.
  ISBN-13: 978-0-531-25039-6 (lib. bdg.)   ISBN-10: 0-531-25039-3 (lib. bdg.)
  ISBN-13: 978-0-531-26564-2 (pbk.)   ISBN-10: 0-531-26564-1 (pbk.)
  1. United States—History—Revolution, 1775–1783—Juvenile literature.
I. Title. II. Series.
  E208.G82 2011
  973.3—dc22   2011016232

All rights reserved. Published in 2012 by Children's Press, an imprint of
Scholastic Inc.
Printed in China 62
SCHOLASTIC, CHILDREN'S PRESS, CORNERSTONES OF FREEDOM™,
and associated logos are trademarks and/or registered trademarks of
Scholastic Inc.

5 6 7 8 9 10 R 21 20 19 18 17 16 15 14 13

Photographs © 2012: Alamy Images/World History Archive: 26; AP Images:
55 (Alfred/SIPA), 51 (Charles Dharapak), 5 bottom, 54 (Hussein Malla);
Architect of the Capitol, Washington, DC/John Trumbull: back cover,
32, 39, 44, 58 bottom; Bridgeman Art Library International Ltd., London/
New York: 57 top (Mather Brown/Boston Athenaeum, USA), 57 bottom
(Charles Willson Peale/The Huntington Library, Art Collections & Botanical
Gardens), 8 (Alfred Pearce/Private Collection/Peter Newark American
Pictures); Corbis Images: 2, 3, 24, 53 bottom; Josh Gregory: 64; Library
of Congress: 4 top, 14 (Paul Revere/Marion S. Carson Collection), 46 (C.
Seiler); Military and Historical Image Bank/Don Troiani/www.histori-
calimagebank.com: 4 bottom, 22; North Wind Picture Archives: 17, 58 top
(Alonzo Chappel), 53 top (John Trumbull), 7, 10, 16, 38, 42 bottom, 42 top, 43,
48, 50, Superstock, Inc.: 30 (Alonzo Chappel), 45 (Thomas Gainsborough),
cover, 34 (Emanuel Gottlieb Leutze/Metropolitan Museum of Art, New York
City), 5 top, 29, 56 (Charles Peale Polk/National Gallery of Art, Washington
DC), 36 (Joshua Reynolds/Frick Collection); The Granger Collection, New
York: 25, 41 (Alonzo Chappel), 23 (John Singleton Copley), 13 (Karl Anton
Hickel), 49 (Howard Pyle), 6, 18, 20, 28, 35, 59.

Did you know that studying history can be fun?

BRING HISTORY TO LIFE by becoming a history investigator. Examine the evidence (primary and secondary source materials); cross-examine the people and witnesses. Take a look at what was happening at the time—but be careful! What happened years ago might suddenly become incredibly interesting and change the way you think!

Contents

SETTING THE SCENE
A New Start in North America 6

CHAPTER 1
Seeds of Rebellion 8

CHAPTER 2
The War Begins 18

CHAPTER 3
The Fight for Freedom 26

CHAPTER 4
Onward to Victory 36

CHAPTER 5
Aftermath 46

MAP OF THE EVENTS
What Happened Where? 52

THE STORY CONTINUES
The Cry for Freedom 54

Influential Individuals 56
Timeline 58
Living History 60
Resources 61
Glossary 62
Index...........................63
About the Author..............64

A New Start in North America

The colonies expanded quickly as businesses found success in the new continent.

In the early 17th century, English **colonists** began settling in North America. Most came to find land and work. They hoped to become successful and wealthy. One of their goals was to expand westward where land

and opportunities were plentiful. Slavery was legal in America at the time. It played an important role in the growth of the colonies, especially in the South.

By the mid-18th century, the settlers had established 13 colonies along North America's Atlantic coast. The colonists were British. They were **subjects** of Great Britain, under the king. Colonists were expected to follow the laws that Parliament made in England.

In 1754, war broke out between France and Great Britain for control of North America. Both sides had Native American allies. The American colonists fought alongside Great Britain. Great Britain won the conflict, known both as the French and Indian War and the Seven Years' War. The victory cost Britain huge sums of money and created the problem of having to govern and protect new lands they won from France.

The French and Indian War was a long and bloody conflict.

AMERICA AT JAMESTOWN IN 1607.

CHAPTER 1

SEEDS OF REBELLION

The British military protected the colonies from Native American attacks along the western frontier.

BRITAIN HAD TO QUICKLY

decide how to govern the new land. Colonists were eager to expand westward. But all the land west of the colonies was Indian territory. Violence between Native Americans and British troops and colonists often occurred along the western edges of the colonies.

Colonists clashed with Native Americans as they attempted to expand westward.

The Proclamation of 1763

Great Britain issued the Proclamation of 1763. The proclamation prevented colonists from settling on Indian land. It also ordered that any colonists currently living on Indian land had to return to colonial soil. All land west of the Appalachian Mountains was proclaimed to be Indian territory. These boundaries were established to halt the flow of American settlers to the west until

Britain could set up a new form of government for the recently acquired lands. Many colonists were unhappy with Britain's decision to limit their movements. They believed Britain did not have the right to **sovereignty** in North America.

Too Many Taxes

To pay off its war **debt**, Great Britain began taxing the American colonies to raise money. The colonists believed the British did not have this right. Great Britain argued that it did hold this sovereign right in the American colonies. Britain had imposed taxes throughout all of its colonial holdings. It assumed it could do so in its American colonies.

In 1764, Parliament issued the Plantation Act, also known as the Sugar Act. This act placed a high **duty** on sugar and molasses **imported** from non-British merchants. The colonists would be forced to purchase all of their sugar and molasses from British merchants.

In 1765, Parliament issued the Stamp Act. Although stamp acts were common in Britain, it angered colonists. The act placed a tax on almost all printed papers, including newspapers, legal documents, and certain kinds of books. These papers could not be issued or sold without special stamps purchased from the British government.

Colonists had no voice in Britain's government because they were not allowed to vote in the British elections. They argued it was unfair for them to

be taxed without representation. Many colonists refused to pay for stamps. Others burned stamps, rioted, and threatened British workers in charge of selling the stamps.

Colonial merchants began refusing to purchase goods from British merchants. British merchants protested to Parliament that the Stamp Act was harming their businesses. In 1766, Parliament **repealed** the tax. But it issued a new act on the same day. The Declaratory Act stated that the British government had the power to tax and make laws for the colonies whenever and however it wished.

In 1767, Parliament issued new acts placing duties on imported goods such as glass, paper, and tea. These acts and several others were known as the Townshend Acts. British officers soon were stationed at colonial ports to make sure the duties were paid. Colonists began **smuggling** goods such as tea into the country so they would not have to pay duties.

The Boston Massacre

In 1768, 4,000 British troops were sent to Boston, Massachusetts. Tensions grew between the colonists and the soldiers.

On March 5, 1770, a barber's **apprentice** named Edward Garrick was sent to collect payment owed by a British officer. When Garrick arrived at the British offices, a guard refused to let him in. The two began arguing and soon drew the attention of nearby colonists.

American colonists were subject to the laws of the British Parliament.

The Boston Massacre was seen as a brutal attack by many colonists.

The colonists joined in the argument and dared the guard to shoot at them. More British soldiers arrived and tried to break up the growing crowd. The colonists menaced the soldiers and hurled objects at them.

One of the British soldiers heard someone yell "Fire!" The confused soldier raised his gun and pulled the trigger, thinking that his captain had shouted the order. Other soldiers heard the shot and began firing their weapons as well. Five people were killed and nine others were injured.

The Boston Tea Party

Parliament repealed most of the Townshend Acts on the day of the Boston Massacre. But the British left the tea duty in place to maintain the principle that Parliament had a right to tax the colonists.

A major London tea supplier called the East India Company lost a lot of business when Americans stopped purchasing its tea. By 1773, the company had 17 million pounds (7.7 million kilograms) of unsold tea in its warehouses. Usually, the company grew its tea in India and shipped it to England. British tea merchants purchased this tea and shipped it to America, where they sold it at higher prices.

In May 1773, Parliament changed this system with the Tea Act. The Tea Act allowed the East India Company to sell its tea directly to the colonists. The goal of the act would be to help the company's business and allow

The Sons of Liberty destroyed thousands of pounds of tea during the Boston Tea Party.

Americans to buy tea at lower prices. It would also hurt smuggling in the area, a major problem for the British, because the Tea Act made British tea cheap and easy to get.

The colonists, however, saw the Tea Act as yet another example of Great Britain taxing them without the right to do so. By the time news of the act reached America, seven East India Company ships were already on their way to Boston. Samuel Adams was among the colonial leaders who wanted to prevent the company from selling its tea. He realized that by accepting the tea, Americans would also be accepting Parliament's right to tax the colonists. He and a group of rebels called the Sons of Liberty began planning a protest.

The ships began arriving in Boston Harbor in late November. The Sons of Liberty guarded the ships so they could not be unloaded. The Sons of Liberty tried to convince British officials to send the ships back. But the

YESTERDAY'S HEADLINES

Most historians today agree that the Boston Massacre was not a massacre but a riot. The British soldiers were in America to enforce laws that the British believed they had the right to enact. Some of the colonists who gathered that day had clubs and knives. Tempers flared, and the British started firing wildly. The event was used by many colonists to turn public opinion against the British. The strategy worked, and the Boston Massacre fueled much of the colonists' hatred toward the king and Parliament.

officials refused. On the night of December 16, 1773, a group of colonists dressed as Mohawk Indians snuck into the harbor and threw the crates of tea into the water.

CHAPTER 2

THE WAR BEGINS

British soldiers kept strict rule over the people of Boston.

IN 1774, PARLIAMENT BEGAN passing a series of laws that came to be known as the Intolerable Acts. These acts were designed to punish Massachusetts for destroying millions of dollars worth of property. Parliament then ordered Boston Harbor to be closed until the colonists paid for the tea they had destroyed. British general Thomas Gage was named governor of Massachusetts. It became illegal for the colonists to hold town meetings or elect their own officials without permission from the British.

The Administration of Justice Act required that any British officials charged with murder be tried for their crimes in England rather than in the colonies. The colonists saw this as a way to legalize any murders committed by British soldiers in the colonies. The acts also saw the return of an unpopular law that allowed British officials to house their troops in colonists' homes.

The First Continental Congress

On September 5, 1774, representatives from 12 of the 13 colonies met in Philadelphia to discuss what should be done in response to the Intolerable Acts. These men called themselves the Continental Congress.

They decided that each of the colonies would be given a single vote in all decisions. They agreed that the colonies should be free from any taxes for which they did not vote. They also agreed that the British military should not be allowed in the colonies without American permission.

They created a document that stated what they believed their rights should be. Among these were the right to hold meetings, the right to a fair trial by

The First Continental Congress organized the patriots' ideas into a single document.

A FIRSTHAND LOOK AT
THE PLAN OF UNION

Some members of the Continental Congress wanted to end tensions with Britain and remain peacefully under British rule. Pennsylvania representative Joseph Galloway created a document called the Plan of Union. The document explained his idea for an American government that would work with the British government to make laws for the colonies. Galloway remained loyal to Britain when the colonists went to war. See page 60 for a link to view the document online.

jury, and the right to own property. The Congress sent the document to King George III in hopes that the British government would agree to the demands. The Continental Congress agreed to stop importing goods from British merchants until the demands were met. They also agreed to stop exporting their own products to the British if the demands were still not met within a year.

Spies and Militias

Local **militias** had existed since the earliest days of the colonies. Many militiamen had fought in the French and Indian War. They began to gather ammunition and other supplies in preparation for conflict with Britain.

Many militiamen were not interested in making peace with Great Britain. In Massachusetts, a network of spies formed under the leadership of Samuel Adams, John

The Battles of Lexington and Concord, in Massachusetts, marked the beginning of the Revolutionary War.

Hancock, and Paul Revere. Revere organized a group whose purpose was to keep an eye on the activities of General Gage.

In April 1775, spies learned that Gage was planning an attack against the rebels. His troops would march toward Lexington, just 12 miles (19 kilometers) northwest of Boston. They planned to arrest Adams and Hancock for **treason**. The troops would then head west to the town of Concord, where militia groups had secretly been storing supplies.

The Battle of Lexington

Thanks to the information from Revere's spy network, the men at Concord hid or destroyed their supplies. They were ready for the British. On April 18, Revere learned that Gage's troops would begin their march later that night.

Revere and his men took no chances in making sure their warning reached Lexington and Concord. He and a friend each set out on horseback toward Lexington. Three other men climbed to the top of a tall church tower and used lanterns to signal riders in the nearby town of Charlestown. The riders alerted other colonists that the British were coming.

The next morning, 700 British soldiers arrived at Lexington and commanded the 77 waiting militiamen to throw down their weapons. The militiamen refused. A shot was fired. It's not clear who fired the first shot. It was likely a colonist shooting from behind a fence. The British returned fire and charged. These were the first shots fired

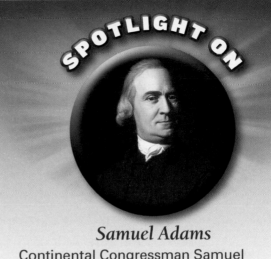

SPOTLIGHT ON

Samuel Adams

Continental Congressman Samuel Adams was one of the most influential American leaders during the Revolutionary War and the years that led up to it. Through his writings and involvement with various organizations, he became one of the leading voices of the growing resistance. After the war, he served as a state senator and governor of Massachusetts.

in the American Revolutionary War. Eight militiamen were killed. Nine others were wounded.

The Battle of Concord

The British marched toward Concord. They still hoped to find and destroy the Americans' hidden weapons. The Concord militia waited for the British across a bridge just north of the town. As the British forces began searching the town, militias from the surrounding areas arrived to join up with their Concord allies.

The British found ammunition and wooden gun carriages. The carriages were frames on which large guns were mounted to be fired. The British tried to burn the carriages. But they accidentally set the town courthouse on fire. The militiamen saw the fire and began marching over the bridge into town. British troops fired warning shots, but the Americans refused to back down. British troops soon began firing at the militiamen.

The British met with significant resistance from the colonists at Concord.

The American troops outnumbered the British and were able to drive them back quickly. But the British forces met resistance as they retreated from Concord. Hundreds of militiamen from as far away as New Hampshire had positioned themselves along the roads back to Boston. They hid on hilltops, behind trees, and in barns. The British had no way to defend themselves against this style of fighting. They quickly marched back to Charlestown.

The victories at Lexington and Concord inspired militias from around the colonies to begin marching toward Boston. Soon, about 15,000 American troops surrounded the city. Gage and 6,500 British soldiers were trapped.

YESTERDAY'S HEADLINES

The American militia at Concord began marching toward the British troops when they saw their town burning. But the fires were purely accidental. British troops even tried to help the townspeople put out the fires. It is possible that before seeing the fires, the militiamen might not have attacked the British. But some historians believe they were ready and willing to fight under any circumstances. The men who fought at Concord were a special group of militiamen known as the minutemen. They were ready to fight at a moment's notice.

CHAPTER 3

THE FIGHT FOR FREEDOM

Even after Lexington and Concord, the Continental Congress still hoped to reconcile differences with Great Britain.

ON MAY 10, 1775, A SECOND Continental Congress came together in Philadelphia. One of its goals was to determine how to conduct the war against Britain. Most representatives were not seeking independence from the British. They were still looking for a solution to the problems between themselves, as British subjects, and Britain.

George Washington proved to be a well-liked and effective military leader.

A New Leader

On June 15, 1775, the Congress appointed George Washington as commander in chief of the new American army, called the Continental army. Washington was a wealthy farmer who had served as an officer in the French and Indian War. He was also a popular politician. Washington quickly began recruiting men and collecting weapons for the Continentals.

The Battle of Bunker Hill

The first major battle of the war occurred just two days after Washington was handed control of the army. Just across the river from Boston, two high hills in Charlestown offered the perfect spot to fire down on the British troops in the city. American colonel William Prescott and his soldiers began **fortifying** the hills, which were known as Breed's Hill and Bunker Hill.

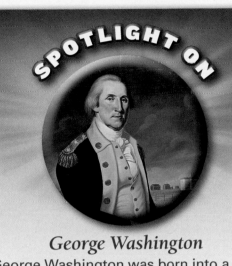

SPOTLIGHT ON

George Washington

George Washington was born into a wealthy family of Virginia plantation owners on February 22, 1732. When he was 22 years old, he was made an officer in the British military and fought in the French and Indian War. Following the American Revolution, Washington played a major role in the creation of the U.S. Constitution. He was elected in 1789 as the first U.S. president.

The Americans built their defenses atop Breed's Hill. British forces began firing cannons from the nearby harbor. The cannon blasts didn't stop the Americans. They continued to build. General Gage realized that the only way to force the Americans off the hills was to send ground troops into battle. He ordered Major General William Howe to attack the hills with 2,300 British soldiers.

The Americans began firing as soon as the British arrived on the northern banks of the river. The British

General Montgomery was killed in the attack on Quebec.

eventually drove the Americans back from the hills, but at great cost. More than 1,000 British soldiers were killed in the attack. The Americans lost 450 soldiers. Even though the British won the battle, the Americans had proved themselves capable fighters. Great Britain soon placed Howe in charge of the British forces. General Gage returned to England.

The Next Battles

In fall 1775, American forces invaded Canada, which was under British rule. American general Richard Montgomery took control of Montreal in early November. He then set out to join his troops with the forces of Benedict Arnold. Montgomery and Arnold attempted to take the city of Quebec. They were unsuccessful.

On February 27, 1776, about 1,000 American militiamen defeated a force of 1,600 **Loyalists** outside Wilmington, North Carolina.

By summer 1776, the Continental Congress had finally decided that it would be impossible for the colonies to remain under British rule. Independence from Britain became America's goal.

The Declaration of Independence

On June 11, 1776, Congress members Thomas Jefferson, Roger Sherman, John Adams, Robert Livingston, and Benjamin Franklin began working on a document that would explain the colonies' reasons for seeking independence.

A FIRSTHAND LOOK AT
THE DECLARATION OF INDEPENDENCE

The Declaration of Independence is one of the most well-known and important documents in U.S. history. The ideas it contains became the foundation of the U.S. government. Since 1952, the one-page document has been on display at the National Archives in Washington, D.C. It is kept in a special airtight case that prevents the paper from decaying. Each year, millions of Americans visit the National Archives to get a look at it. See page 60 for a link to view the document online.

The Declaration of Independence was approved on July 4, 1776.

The Declaration of Independence was written mainly by Jefferson. It stated, "Governments are instituted among men, deriving their just powers from the consent of the governed." Because Great Britain had never asked consent of the colonists before passing laws for them, the Americans believed that it was their right to separate and form their own government. On July 2, the Congress voted to declare independence. Two days later, they approved the Declaration of Independence as their official statement.

Attack on New York

Great Britain sent Admiral Richard Howe, brother of William Howe, to America with a fleet of ships and 34,000 soldiers. The Howes were to meet with American leaders and demand that they surrender. The officers offered **pardons** to the Americans if they would end the conflict. The Americans refused, and the Howes began making plans to capture New York.

On August 27, General Howe landed troops on Long Island, New York. He was quickly able to force Washington's army west from Brooklyn into Manhattan. Two weeks later, Howe moved his troops into Manhattan. By October, he had pushed Washington north into the nearby town of White Plains.

The Battle of White Plains

Washington left behind two **garrisons**. He hoped that they would slow down Howe's pursuit. The first was at Fort Lee, across the Hudson River to the west of Manhattan. The other was at Fort Washington, in northern Manhattan. Howe's forces slipped between the garrisons and chased Washington into White Plains. Washington lost the battle. He was once again forced to withdraw northward with his 14,000 troops.

Poor weather prevented Howe from following. He turned back toward Manhattan and set his sights on Fort Washington. On November 20, British general Charles Cornwallis took over Fort Lee and began driving Washington's troops southwest across New Jersey. By late December, Washington had been forced across the Delaware River. The Continental army now had only 6,000 troops. Howe and Cornwallis began settling down for the winter, when fighting usually slowed down. They left their men at posts along the eastern side of the Delaware River.

The Battles of Trenton and Princeton

Washington knew that only 1,400 British troops guarded the city of Trenton, New Jersey, on the eastern banks of the Delaware. On December 25, 1776,

Washington's surprise attack in New Jersey proved to be extremely effective.

Washington launched a surprise attack across the icy river with 4,200 American soldiers. The Americans easily overtook the British forces. They moved on to take Trenton the next day.

On January 2, 1777, General Cornwallis arrived at Trenton with 8,000 troops. He attacked, but Washington cleverly snuck away westward. Late that night, Washington began moving his men north toward Princeton.

The next morning, Washington's army defeated the British forces at Princeton. This cleared a path to move northward to the town of Morristown. There, Washington was able to settle in for the winter and begin rebuilding his army.

TODAY'S PERSPECTIVE

George Washington was chosen to be the commander in chief of the Continental army for his military abilities and commitment to the cause of colonial freedom. The Second Continental Congress also hoped that choosing a wealthy farmer from Virginia would tie the southern colonies more closely to the rebellion. Washington increased the length of time soldiers would serve, equipped his men, and molded the rebels into a professional army. Most historians agree that the Continental army would not have defeated the British without Washington's leadership.

CHAPTER 4

ONWARD TO VICTORY

John Burgoyne helped lead
the British attack on New
England in 1777.

GREAT BRITAIN VIEWED

New England as the center of the Americans' power. British leaders began planning ways to cut it off from the rest of the colonies. When winter passed, British general John Burgoyne began moving south from Canada toward New York, where he joined forces with General Howe.

The American forces were unable to hold their ground at the Battle of the Brandywine, in Pennsylvania.

Brandywine and Saratoga

In July 1777, General Howe left Burgoyne and his men to hold New York. Howe began moving south toward Pennsylvania, where he planned to take Philadelphia. On September 11, he defeated Washington at Brandywine Creek, just 25 miles (40 km) outside of Philadelphia. But Howe's decision to take Philadelphia was a costly mistake.

About the same time that General Howe had set off for Philadelphia, Burgoyne went on the offensive. He captured the American forts Ticonderoga and Edward in July and then moved on to make camp in the town of Saratoga. Burgoyne planned to move his troops south and take the city of Albany. But General Horatio Gates was camped nearby with a growing American force.

The two sides clashed on September 19. Gates's forces were able to hold back the British. Burgoyne was forced to withdraw. In early October, Burgoyne took 1,500 soldiers and attempted to circle around the side of the American army. The British were quickly defeated, and Gates began using his massive army to surround the main British camp. Burgoyne was forced to surrender several days later.

Burgoyne's surrender was a major victory for the Americans.

New Friends

As winter approached, Washington settled his troops at Valley Forge, near Philadelphia. The weather was harsh and food was scarce. But good news was soon on its way.

During a **diplomatic** visit to France, Benjamin Franklin and Silas Deane heard about an experienced German soldier named Friedrich Wilhelm von Steuben. They hired him to go to America to train Washington's forces at Valley Forge. Steuben taught them how to use their weapons properly and march in formation. He even wrote a manual that the American military would use as a guide for many years.

General Gates's victory over General Burgoyne encouraged France to join the cause for American independence. France had already been secretly providing money and supplies to the American forces. In 1778, the country officially declared war and began sending ships and troops to America. Other countries soon followed France's lead. Spain entered the war in 1779, and the Netherlands joined in 1780.

A FIRSTHAND LOOK AT
STEUBEN'S *REGULATIONS*

Baron von Steuben's *Regulations for the Order and Discipline of the Troops of the United States* was an important guide in the early years of the U.S. military. While it is no longer used, many of its basic ideas are still important to modern military tactics. See page 60 for a link to view the book online.

Baron von Steuben improved the American forces with his training exercises.

The Americans' new allies had the resources to compete with Great Britain's huge fleet of ships. Combined with the American naval forces, they were able to keep the British busy at sea. They attacked ships off the British coasts and kept them from sailing to America.

Nathanael Greene

Before joining the military, Nathanael Greene spent many years as a member of the Rhode Island colonial legislature. He joined the Rhode Island army in 1775 and became a general a year later. Greene served directly under General Washington during the early years of the war. He was present at such conflicts as the Siege of Boston and Washington's battles across New York and New Jersey.

In 1778, Greene was made commander of the southern army. He successfully held the British forces back from conquering North Carolina and defended the southern colonies throughout the rest of the war.

The Battle of Guilford Courthouse

By early 1781, the American forces had proper training, manpower, and powerful allies. On March 15, General Nathanael Greene brought 4,500 American troops together at Guilford Courthouse in Greensboro, North Carolina. General

The American forces drove back Cornwallis at Guilford Courthouse.

Thousands of American troops surrounded Cornwallis's forces at Yorktown, Virginia.

Cornwallis and fewer than 2,000 British troops attacked. The Americans caused major damage to Cornwallis's forces while losing few men themselves. Rather than take any unnecessary losses, Greene withdrew.

The Siege of Yorktown

On August 1, Cornwallis and his men arrived in Yorktown, Virginia. Cornwallis hoped to rest his men and get additional supplies before continuing. Almost immediately, spies working under French general Lafayette saw that Cornwallis was settling in for a long stay.

Cornwallis's surrender began to bring the war to a close.

Lafayette told Washington about Cornwallis. Washington learned about the same time that a fleet of French ships and 3,000 soldiers would soon be arriving in the Chesapeake Bay. On August 19, the combined forces of Washington and French general Rochambeau began marching toward Virginia. Ten days later, the French fleet arrived at Chesapeake Bay. Meanwhile, Cornwallis waited for British general Henry Clinton to arrive with more troops and supplies.

The American and French forces arrived at Williamsburg, Virginia, on September 20. Eight days later, they marched on Yorktown and began planning ways to get past Cornwallis's defenses. Over the next several weeks, the allied forces beat down Cornwallis. They cut off his supply routes as he continued to wait for Clinton's arrival.

By October 16, Cornwallis knew that Clinton would not arrive in time to fend off the allied attackers. He attempted to escape with his surviving forces but was foiled by a heavy rainstorm. He officially surrendered on October 19.

Though some fighting continued, the war was essentially over. News of Cornwallis's defeat reached England a little more than a month after the surrender. Upon hearing the news, the British prime minister described the situation simply and correctly: "Oh, God, it is all over."

SPOTLIGHT ON

Charles Cornwallis
Born in 1738, Cornwallis enlisted in the British military when he was 18 years old. He fought in Europe during the Seven Years' War (1756–1763). He inherited his father's seat as a member of Parliament when he returned to England. Cornwallis often sided with the colonists' requests. He even voted against the Stamp Act and the Intolerable Acts. After returning to England at the end of the war, Cornwallis was made governor-general of India, which was at the time controlled by Great Britain. Later, he served as viceroy, or colonial ruler, of Ireland. He died in 1805.

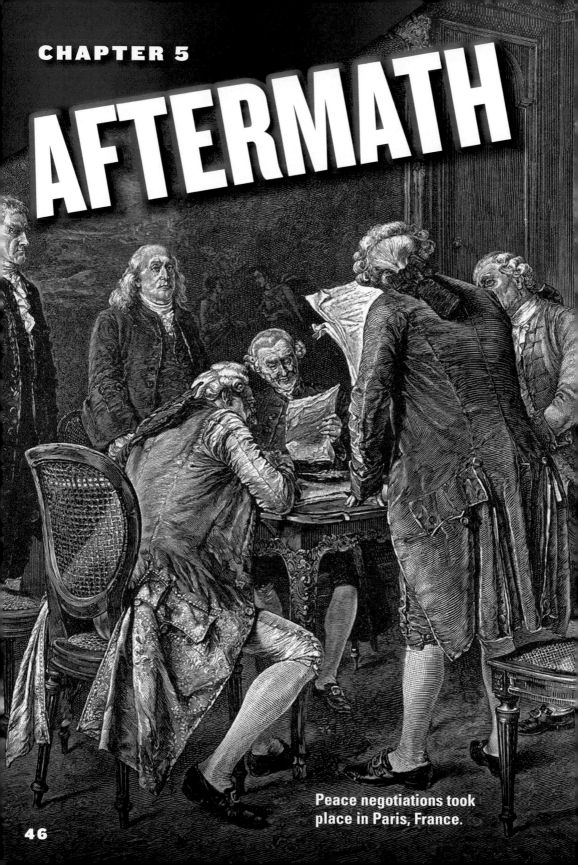

CHAPTER 5

AFTERMATH

Peace negotiations took place in Paris, France.

THE ALLIED FORCES HAD ACHIEVED a hard-won victory over Great Britain. On February 28, 1782, Great Britain agreed to begin negotiations to formally end the war. In April, representatives from America and Great Britain met in Paris, France, to discuss the terms of peace for a treaty.

Benjamin Franklin (in background) was among the American negotiators sent to Paris.

The Treaty of Paris

The Americans chose John Adams, Benjamin Franklin, and John Jay to be their negotiators. The three men had two main goals to accomplish in the treaty. First, Great Britain had to recognize America as a free

A FIRSTHAND LOOK AT
THE TREATY OF PARIS

Like many other important historical documents, the original Treaty of Paris is today located at the National Archives in Washington, D.C. You can view it in person or see page 60 for a link to view the document online.

and independent nation. Second, any boundaries preventing American expansion to the west would have to be removed. Borders for the newly formed American nation were set at the Mississippi River to the west, Canada to the north, and Florida to the south. Great Britain kept ownership of Canada and returned

Loyalists were forced out of the country after the war.

A VIEW FROM ABROAD

Most Americans wanted independence. But some people stayed loyal to Great Britain throughout the entire war. Many of the Loyalists were enslaved people who had escaped from their American owners. Many even fought as part of the British military. These Loyalists were treated poorly after the war. Other Americans were unwilling to forgive them for siding with the enemy. About 100,000 Loyalists left America. Most of them moved to Canada or England.

With the war over, American soldiers were able to return to their homes.

Florida back to the Spanish after having gained it in the Seven Years' War.

On September 3, 1783, the American negotiators once again met in Paris. They signed the final version of the Treaty of Paris. The war was officially over. The last British military forces in America left from New York City on November 25.

A Nation Is Born

Each of the 13 colonies had its own laws and government. When the colonies became states, each one continued to govern itself. This principle reflected the ideas in the Declaration of Independence. Americans would not be governed by faraway rulers. Instead, they would vote for local leaders who could voice their wishes to a central government.

In 1787, leaders from each of the states came together in Philadelphia. They created the U.S. Constitution. This document organized a federal government in which each state was fairly represented. This document has served the country for more than 200 years. It has continually granted new freedoms and rights to Americans.

TODAY'S PERSPECTIVE

Today, it might be difficult to imagine Great Britain and the United States as enemies. The relationship between the two countries was understandably rocky for the first few decades following the Revolutionary War. But they have been close allies since the early 20th century. During World War I (1914–1918), they fought on the same side for the first time. Since then, they have been allies in every major conflict that either has been involved in.

What Happened Where?

The Battles of Trenton and Princeton After losing several battles in the previous months, George Washington was able to successfully attack the British and bring his army back from the edge of defeat.

The Siege of Yorktown The Siege of Yorktown was the decisive battle of the war. By defeating British general Charles Cornwallis, American and French allies struck a crippling blow to the British military.

SC

GA

CANADA

MA

NH

Concord

MA

Bunker Hill

Lexington

NY

CT

RI

PA

NJ

Princeton

Trenton

MD

DE

ATLANTIC
OCEAN

VA

Yorktown

NC

The Battle of Bunker Hill The first major battle of the war took place on the outskirts of Boston as the American forces attempted to subdue the British army trapped in the city. The Americans caused heavy damage before withdrawing, proving that they could hold their own against the well-trained British military.

The Battles of Lexington and Concord The first shots of the American Revolution were fired at these battles. Tensions were finally pushed to the limit when the American militias thought they saw British troops burning the town of Concord.

N
W E
S

| 0 | 150 | 300 mi |
| 0 | 150 | 300 km |

☐ 13 Colonies
✷ Battle sites

The Cry for Freedom

In 2011, Libyan protestors called for leader Muammar Qaddafi to step down.

In the years since the American Revolution, many other countries have fought for the freedom to govern themselves. Some of these revolutions have been violent,

SEVERAL PROTESTING EGYPTIANS SET

just as the American Revolution was. Others were achieved with the use of more peaceful methods.

In 2011, the people of Egypt rose up in protest against President Hosni Mubarak. Mubarak had ruled the country for almost 30 years. The people voiced their unhappiness with Mubarak's leadership using demonstrations and strikes. He was forced to resign. Similar uprisings occurred in Libya, Tunisia, and other Middle Eastern countries around the same time. Even today, the spirit of revolution is alive.

Protestors in Egypt forced President Hosni Mubarak out of office.

THEMSELVES ON FIRE IN 2011.

INFLUENTIAL INDIVIDUALS

Benjamin Franklin (1706–1790) helped write the Declaration of Independence and served as a diplomat in France during the war.

Thomas Gage (1721–1787) was commander in chief of the British army in America from 1763 to 1775.

Samuel Adams (1722–1803) was a politician who helped organize early resistance to British tax laws and later served on the Continental Congress.

Jean-Baptiste-Donatien de Vimeur, Comte de Rochambeau (1725–1807) was a French general who helped win the war by joining forces with George Washington at the Siege of Yorktown.

William Howe (1729–1814) was the commander in chief of the British army in America from 1776 to 1778.

Baron Friedrich Wilhelm von Steuben (1730–1794) was a German officer hired to train the American forces in proper military tactics.

George Washington

George Washington (1732–1799) was the leader of the Continental army during the revolution and later became the first U.S. president.

Paul Revere (1735–1818) was a patriot from Boston who helped establish spy and messenger networks in the colonies.

John Adams (1735–1826) was a politician who served on the Continental Congress, helped negotiate the Treaty of Paris, and became the second U.S. president.

John Adams

John Hancock (1737–1793) was an American patriot who served in the Continental Congress.

Charles Cornwallis (1738–1805) was a British general whose defeat at Yorktown brought about the end of the war.

King George III (1738–1820) was the king of Great Britain during the American Revolution.

Thomas Jefferson (1743 1826) was an American politician who served in the Continental Congress, helped write the Declaration of Independence, and became the third U.S. president.

Thomas Jefferson

Marie-Joseph-Paul-Yves-Roch-Gilbert du Motier, Marquis de Lafayette (1757–1834) was a French general who assisted at the Siege of Yorktown.

TIMELINE

1765

March 22
Stamp Act passed

1770

March 5
Boston Massacre

1773

December 16
Boston Tea Party

1777

September 11
Battle of Brandywine
Creek

September 19
Battle of Saratoga

1778

France enters the war

1779

Spain enters the war

1774

September 5
First Continental Congress meets in Philadelphia

1775

April 19
Battles of Lexington and Concord

June 15
George Washington appointed commander in chief of the Continental army

June 17
Battle of Bunker Hill

1776

July 4
Second Continental Congress approves the Declaration of Independence

October
Battle of White Plains

December 25
Washington crosses the Delaware River

1780

The Netherlands enters the war

1781

March 15
Battle of Guilford Courthouse

October 19
General Cornwallis surrenders at Yorktown

1783

September 3
Treaty of Paris signed

LIVING HISTORY

Primary sources provide firsthand evidence about a topic. Witnesses to a historical event create primary sources. They include autobiographies, newspaper reports of the time, oral histories, photographs, and memoirs. A secondary source analyzes primary sources, and is one step or more removed from the event. Secondary sources include textbooks, encyclopedias, and commentaries.

The Declaration of Independence The declaration is a formal explanation of why the colonies declared independence from Great Britain. The document can be viewed at *www.archives.gov/exhibits /charters/declaration.html*

Joseph Galloway's Plan of Union Pennsylvanian Joseph Galloway suggested the creation of an American parliament. You can see it at *http://press-pubs.uchicago.edu/founders/documents /v1ch7s3.html*

Paul Revere's Engraving of the Boston Massacre Revere's engraving fueled Americans' anger and was seen by thousands of colonists. The original engraving can be found at *www.loc.gov /pictures/resource/ppmsca.01657/*

Regulations for the Order and Discipline of the Troops of the United States The Continental Congress approved Baron von Steuben's military handbook for use by the army. The book can be viewed at *http://books.google.com/books?id=KjNFAAAAYAAJ&prints ec=frontcover#v=onepage&q&f=false*

The Treaty of Paris The treaty formally ended the war between America and Great Britain. A copy of the treaty can be viewed at *www.ourdocuments.gov/doc.php?flash=true&doc=6#*